A Most Marvelous Piece of Luck

A Most Marvelous Piece of Luck

Greg Williamson

WAYWISER

First published in 2008 by

THE WAYWISER PRESS

Bench House, 82 London Road, Chipping Norton, Oxon OX7 5FN, UK
P.O. Box 6205, Baltimore, MD 21206, USA
http://waywiser-press.com

Editor-in-Chief
Philip Hoy

Senior American Editor
Joseph Harrison

Associate Editors
Clive Watkins   Greg Williamson

A CIP catalogue record for this book is available from the British Library

Hardback ISBN
978-1-904130-30-7

Paperback ISBN
978-1-904130-28-4

Printed and bound by
T. J. International Ltd., Padstow, Cornwall

Acknowledgements

The author wishes to thank the editors of the following journals and anthologies in whose pages these poems first appeared: *32 Poems*: "Criticism," "Easter Island," "Rock," and "School"; *Backwards City Review*: "Sex" and "Sex"; *Nebraska Review*: "College," "Hat," "Home," "Paper," and "Scissors"; *Smartish Pace*: "Clouds," "Man," "Snow," "Weather," and "Woman"; *Sonnets*: "Fire"; *Unsplendid*: "Beer," "Feet," "Hands," "Mega-Tsunami," "Music," "Mountains," and "The Ten Spacetime Dimensional Universe"; *Yale Review*: "Space" and "Time."

Contents

Contents

– What happen then, Mr. Bones?
– I had a most marvellous   piece of luck. I died.

– John Berryman

... 'Tis a consummation
Devoutly to be wished.

– William Shakespeare

– Damn, they killed Kenny.
– Bastards.

– South Park

Time

for John Hollander

Time was, it wasn't. "Then," a singularity,
Planck's constant, quantum foam, the bottom quark –
Better let them tell it – and, presto, we
Had time. Thus, gnomons, Stonehenge, Harrison's clock.

Time had a future. Time was *in*! And you
Could make it, save it, spend it, even un-
derestimate it (time is money, son?
Sure, but this ain't the time your father knew)

Until your limo slides up to the high
Society grand ball, everyone's there,
Tripping the tarantella (*"merci*, with lime"),
The old soft shoe, high hat, a final air
Under the Milky Way, the signs, the sky-
light's stars, where everything is done

in time.

Space

Space dons Time's Delta pin. First date. Sparks fly.
There's chemistry, there's calculus, there's luck.
And then (and there) there's us, the loinsome fry
Of good old Father Time and Mother Fuck,

Their spacey, new-age offspring, have her face,
His hands, cut from the same cloth, their heirloom.
We're graviton, Calabi-Yau. We're Space
And Time's. We're leg-, head-, elbow-, living *room*,

Until one day there's no room left of you,
Down in the module in your last space suit,
Doing some fieldwork in that dusty place –
Wormholes, dark matter, phase – a firsthand view
Under the Fox, the Swan, the Herdsman's boot,
The Works, where Time keeps keeping time
                                        with Space.

Stars

White dwarfs, red giants, novas, binaries –
Sagan would say beyond the three or four
Stars we still see are billions more that these
Nights twinkle purely in dead metaphor,

And though you wished upon them, reached for them,
You played – without the looks, the lines, the knife-
Like wit – a walk-on cast as "Ibidem,"
An extra in the movie of your life,

Until ("the *reticence*, the use of *gesture*!")
You land the role of a lifetime, dark, sublime,
An in-depth study worthy of film noir's
Late, leading men, in which you readjust your
View of stardom and sidereal time
And see your trophy swept
                              beneath the stars.

Sun

Sometimes mistaken for a UFO,
The plain, G2 main sequence star we call
The "sun" and central to the helio-
centricity we humans almost all

(Despite the Pope's reaction to the news)
In our mean neck of Via Lactea
Accept is toted by Apollo, whose
Plumb gnarly lute chops crush your tra la la

Until you change your tune there, Sunshine, pawn
Your Panpipes for a small beach towel-sized spot
On the green lea to watch the Master stun
The crowd with killer light shows and the lawn
Fill up with "melodies unheard of," hot
Lead licks, fills, flash, like nothing
                                    knew under the sun.

Moon

Diana, Cynthia, Artemis, the moon
Was once, for lovers, loonies, and póetícs,
The symbol of choice – muse, midnight rant, or swoon,
Or moonstruck femme fatale in forties flicks –

Then *dude walked on the moon* (sure he did (wink))
With a two wood and a cart, a golfonaut
Taking a stroke (that's *moxie!*), but you think
The new moon's less romantic than you thought,

Until you lie down in that moonlit vale –
Flowers, cool stones, deep droughts of *poesy*,
Watching armadas of nightclouds and the luna
Moth's looped, signature lunettes – and sail
Along on the smooth Sea of Tranquility
And its eternal footman
                               in the moon.

Earth

Bipolar, plump around the middle, Ma
Was Ma, homemaker, Terra, firm but fair,
With cool pets – entellus, spoonbill, agama –
And a green thumb. We kind of liked it there.

Course then we drilled, drained, scorched, and smoked her out –
Centralia, Copper Basin. No wonder she's hot
(It's a mall world after all), watching some lout
Sinking her fortune in a parking lot

Until, blithe prodigal son, you move back home
To a one-bed basement in suburbia
(Your *old room?* (close)) and questions of self-worth,
As you bunk down to watch, in monochrome,
The farms get bought, Romes burn, gods die like Ra,
In trailers for the latest show
on Earth.

Fire

Imagine that first fire, the doubletakes
Among the vegans, cold, dark, wet: Cave guy
Strikes flint and, boom, you're grilling mammoth steaks,
You're holding hands, you're hooking up, you're dry,

And (years of R&D) it catches on,
Brick ovens, candlelight, of course appalling
Losses, but still, fondue, filet mignon,
And the three-alarm, fanned fire of your first calling

Until there's no more call for you, you box
Up your life's work, archive the ardencies,
The once hot, test-tube topics, and retire
To country climes, keeping an eye on the phlox
In your old field, avuncular now, at peace
With not quite having set the world
                                    on fire.

Water

Distillation of Body (class in awe):
It boils down to vapors, truancy,
And chemicals like hardon, moron, straw,
And varying amounts of irony,

But mostly we're made of water, bottled sweat –
Watery eyes, watery mouths, a stream
Of invective, a river of lies – we're just all wet,
And you've got a head like a lake, you're liquid dream

Until, blue wavelets glinting like doubloons,
You demonstrate the swan dive's "brilliant bow,"
Your backstroke's clean technique ("he's a regular otter"),
Hobnobbing in gin-tinctured afternoons,
Making a statement in your chic maillot,
Another one whose name is writ
                              in water.

Ice

By "ice," we're usually talking H2O
Ice, water ice, the ice of icebergs, ice
Cubes, ice packs, and the iceries of snow
Embroidering a window, you know, *ice*,

But you're in traffic, gloomy, going no-
where, thinking about the slushy road, and work,
Racking up overtime toward the ice floe
Of forced retirement, an old pro clerk,

Until the ceremonial parade
Opens the Winter Games and your event,
The luge, where your sangfroid, self-sacrifice –
Snow-capped, flat on your back, *stylin'* – have made
A legend of you, in your element,
Your own world, fearless, the coolest cat
                                        on ice.

Snow

"A nonequilibrium phenomena"
And "highly non-linear unstable free boundary
Problem," a snowflake, silent as a schwa,
Its fractal lacework cast in free-fall's foundry,

"Records the history of all the ... weather"
It encountered till the double-hung
Panes frame its fall and you recall that feather
And just how long it lasted on your tongue

Until one day you look up from the rime
And you're snowed in, Snow Bunny, play the tape
Of snow days, sled runs, forts, and mistletoe,
Back to a dark den in the wintertime
And metaphor's first flurries' dazzling crepe,
When static on Pop's old TV
                              was snow.

Rain

Sun woke up this morning, had them Georgia blues,
Sungod woke up this morning, had them Georgia blues,
Looked over in the driveway, godson had them too,

```
---------------------------------------
---------------------------------------
-7---7-7---7-7---7-7---7-7\5---5------
-----------------------------7-----7--
---------------------------------------
---------------------------------------
```

So you're garage-bound, sitting on a bucket,
Watching the bubbles ride the blue veneer
Of two-stroke gasoline and thinking, "Fuck it,
Rilke's right, you better switch to beer,"

Until, in one last bluesy singalong,
You're "going up the country (Baby, do
You want to go?)," your basic, anonymous swain
Lamenting how brief those bubbles and how long
The gold, archaic craft that should shine through
The littlest song, so small rains down
                                        can rain.

Wind

You wanna run a windjammer, you'll need wind,
And wind is simply air that's flowing from
High pressure zones to lower ones to find
Its atmospheric equilibrium,

But you're in the doldrums, Cap'n Clerk, the old
Horse latitudes, dead in the water, filling
The logbook in with logs, counting the gold
Coin, snapping the Cap'n's spyglass open, milling,

Until Fate smiles, winds change, you raise the sheets
And plot a course for home and heartland, leave
The sea, the salt, the circling, dorsal-finned,
Bloodthirsty hammerheads to stick your feets
In terra firma, landlubber on reprieve,
Mothballed, dry-docked, and safely
                                    away from the wind.

Ocean

In addition to thermohaline circulation,
The ocean provides for foraminifers,
Which turn to limestone and in their shell formation
Also keep Earth from burning up, or worse,

But you're in boyhood's white chalk caves, its land-
Locked mysteries, dreaming of unexplored
Seacoasts and schooners and ports o' call as you stand
At the board and write, "I will not write on the board,"

Until (how evasive your humor) "'Come,' purred the clays
And gravels," and you go down the adit hole,
A fine white noise replaces the commotion,
And in your grotto, in its passageways,
In your etched stone – put your ear to it, Muster Mole,
Put your ear to it – you can hear
                                    the ocean.

Clouds

Containing only .035%
Of the Earth's fresh water at any given moment,
Clouds are a pretty insubstantial pageant
Really, which the nineteenth century docent

And Englishman, Luke Howard, classified
As stratus, cirrus, nimbus, and cumulus
(From Gr. *flat*, *fruity*, *agile*, and *big-thighed*)
(And every silver lining has one, Gus)

Until, at length, you notice overhead
"Soft coral reefs and powdery tumuli,"
The "grand confections" literalism shrouds
In secrecy, your feet on the ground and your head,
Etymologically speaking ("I
See a bunny"), you old daydreamer,
                                          in the clouds.

Weather

Woolly bears, red skies, bones ... then, *supercomputers*.
Now we would tell the weather, plug in the data –
Isobars, dewpoints, vectors, "thermal polluters" –
Rap on the screen and punch up a sunny day.

Ah, but the weather was wiser. You couldn't tell
It anything. The Lorenz Attractor shows
The merest instability may swell
To storms, long days of rain, depressions, lows,

Until, having weathered it all, slogged on, you cast
Off for some R&R, a long, slow cruise
In the subtropics – swims in the altogether,
Mahogany trim, the Southerly Trades, a last,
Suave waltz under Polaris, Betelgeuse –
Down in your berth, a wee bit
                                    under the weather.

Trees

For trees came crowding where the poet sang,
Bayberry for soap, Sweet Birch for wintergreen,
Black Wattle for the homing boomerang,
The whiskey-aging Oak, tart Mescalbean,

Cork good for bats, Witch-hazel used to dowse,
Sweetbay for catching beavers, scented Fir,
Walnut for gunstocks, bows from the Osage boughs,
Cinchona, Wormwood, salubrious Juniper,

Until eftstoone "the Cypresse funeralle,"
And you drop anchor in "the sayling Pine"
("Sleepe after toyle, port after stormie seas")
To recall the feudal origins of "windfall"
And hear snow crashing in the timberline
And remix tapes of birdsong
                              in the trees.

Garden

"God Almighty first planted a Garden; and
Indeed, it is the purest of human Pleasures,
The greatest Refreshment to the Spirit of Man,"
Said Francis Bacon, and among your treasures –

Wilt, rust, sawflies, cankerworm invasions –
You've seem to have found a troupe of fire ants,
Uncommonly toxic, walking conflagrations,
Who've made you Queen of the Anaphylactic Dance

Until (*Hortus conclusus*, Buttercup!)
Some final spadework as the snowsies come,
And you go dormant to feel the hard freeze harden,
To feed the lawn and push the daisies up
And tend, you *jardiniste*, you old green thumb,
In this the best of all possible worlds,
                                    your garden.

Man

XY, men: Man, but it turns out the Y
One is disintegrating ("tough luck, hon"),
And genderologers predict we'll die
Out, oh, end of the year, *finito*, done,

And there you are, the last man left alive,
Hangdog, dog-tired, plumb tuckered out, so many
Women needing a jar lid loosed or live-
Ass spider squarshed (and still not getting any)

Until you join that ritzy Country Club,
Admiring the lawn ("Bermuda grass or fescue?"),
And stretch out on the faithful, old divan
For the long, upcoming season, grab some grub,
Some shuteye ("Couch Potato to the rescue"),
Your typical, drowsy, heroic,
                              American man.

Woman

XX, kiss kiss, but one X shy of poison
("Watch it, mister!"), but isn't that the point?
Succubus, maiden, famine and foison,
Idealized, feared, bewitching and witch, "aroint

Thee," "love me" – that's the *men's* mag, worn, dogeared,
Who might, on this point only, be excused
As merely adolescents with a beard,
Blustery, horny, and utterly confused

Until, single at long last, liberated,
You get that makeover you've been meaning to,
Mud mask, new makeup, new perfume, a room in
Fashionable Club Dead (#1 rated),
Relaxing, dreaming of ponies, pampering *you*,
And starting to feel
                    like a totally new woman.

Sex

Right then, some words on Procreationist Science:
When a man and a woman (for simplicity's sake)
Form a mutual, one might say, *alliance*,
The man inserts – or, rather, the woman may take

The man's – at any rate, the man's spermatozoa,
Or motile gametes, swim the channel of the
Woman's, let's just say, the woman's ova
Office – right then, quite natural really, lovely,

Until you crash in your new bachelor pad,
The one-room Love Shack, in your leisure suit
To reminisce about the fairer ex-,
Babes at the pool, the trysts you seldom had
Out in the garden of forbidden fruit
Where you have wound up having to pay

for sex.

Sex

Is that right, Dr. Kinsey? Doc, we're talking
The *nasty* – grabass, nookie, *hysteria*
Libidinosa, pop goes the weasel, parking
The dog, ball, bop, bang, wham bam – *copula*,

When human beings dispense with all decorum,
Legs in the air, moan, curse, sweat, squeeze, and straddle
Each other in elevators, haylofts, dorm rooms,
Motels, backstairs, backseats, and back in the saddle

Until you cruise into that singles' bar,
Primped, slick, flashing your pearly whites in *Club
Eternity*, last of the discotheques,
A bonafide playa, into the shrooms and star-
dust, keeping it real, sweet thang, in the deep sub-
culture, where there is nothing at all
                              like sex.

DNA

If Natural Selection "rigidly
Destroys injurious variation" in
The complex codes of A, G, C, and T,
How's Darwin gonna splain the Windsor Chin…

Or *you*(!), the Afterthought, the *Also-Ran*
In life's genetic bouillabaisse – six-fingered,
Stared at, touched with ten-foot poles – who began
In "Last," lost ground, gave into, and malingered

Until the babbling replications cave
And you start talking, garrulously, turkey –
The ABCs of FUBAR, T&A,
IMHO – and taking to the grave
The only extant copy of your quirky,
Rare, self-mocking, murderous
                              DNA?

Baby

Rug rats, ankle biters, *enfants terribles*,
They come from homunculi, the little men
In sperm, where they were *just fine* till some dweeb
Summons his militia, his *minute*men,

Who stumble around for awhile till this one guy,
A caterwauling little gastronome,
Emerges ("Daddy drinks because you cry")
Who grows up and puts daddy in a home,

Until, wrapped up in swaddling coat and tie,
Chrome-domed all over again, a slim peacekeeping
Unit of one, you get a new womb, shady
And quaint, humming an old-time lullaby,
"Momma's gonna buy you a mockingbird," and sleeping,
Or doing a fair impression,
                                    like a baby.

Marriage

With more spouse farms, shrink rap, and psychosprawl
Than you can shake a "stick it" at, you'd say
The All-American marriages are all
Uniquely bad in exactly the same way,

The nagging, shrill, can't-decide-what's-she's-wearing wife
And the gruff, unaffectionate husband who ignores
Her ("these or – ?" "time, dear" "jackass" "you ruined my life"
"My mother is coming" "shoot me" "finish your chores")

Until, eventually, you settle down
And get divorced – from married *life*, that is –
She gets the house, you get a bunk in steerage
Aboard *That Ship Has Sailed* – it's all over town,
What her attorney will refer to as
An irreconcilable difference
                                    in the marriage.

Law

The Law, the Legal *System*, Judicial Mode
(*enrichum lawyericulum*), progressed
Through *Lex Romana*, Magna Carta, *Code
Napoléon*, to Modern Law, the best

System of avarice, show trial, sham
Defense, and justice for all who can buy it, ours,
Where everyone sues and teams of hairpieces cram
The courts with bullshit, Armani, and billable hours

Until you make your closing argument,
Your last ambulance chased, case closed, recess,
And to your paneled study, then, withdraw,
Bury your nose in pandects, precedent,
Cold case notes, seeking damages, redress,
Habeas Corpus, Esq., Attorney
                            at Law.

School

In ancient Roman times, a "pedagogue,"
Or barefoot slave, accompanied a lad,
Or *puer*, guiding him through dialogue
("What is the nature of goodness?"), toga-clad

And strigiled, which evolved in our own youth
To high school, a Ritalin-ed, unrefereed,
Book-bagged, bad-haired, Socratic search for truth
("Does she put out?" "Dude, you got any weed?"),

Until your black tie class reunion, chance
To show them – thinner, strong-jawed – how you fared,
The Queen, the Geek, the Poser, and the Tool,
Under the disco ball, the *senior* dance,
Old friend, old valedictorian, prepared
For this by everything you learned
                                    in school.

College

"Bear with me, gentlemen," as once was billed
By Cardinal Newman (John, H.), "college campus"
Derives from the Latin *collegium* (a guild,
Fraternity, or gathering) and *campus*

(Field), a gathering in a field – *football*,
Crisp, beer-buzzed, ribs-on-the-smoker Saturdays,
Bourbon and bombshells, "Goddamn, boys, it's *football*!"
(Bryant, Paul Bear), boys crying, girls agaze,

Until you suit up for your last home game
And take the field, everyone stands, your great
Career is over – take a bow, son, acknowledge
The crowd – the play-by-play man calls your name,
But you need a miracle, it's fourth and fate,
As you rerun the plays you made
                              in college.

Books

Distinguished in length and form from magazine
Or tract, books as we think of them today
Began with Guttenberg in the fourteen
Hundreds, and his achievement's given way

To pitched battles between the cook- and diet
Books, self-helps and bodice-rippers, lazy,
Plot-lined *New York Times*ers, and the quiet
Excellence of mid-list MFAs

Until you come to that last page, *in me –* ,
Hey, wait a – the gumshoe doesn't apprehend,
The hero doesn't get the girl, the crooks
Aren't caught, Shane isn't coming back, but see,
Right there, in big, block lettering, "THE END,"
Something you had read about
                                              in books.

Criticism

In modern criticism the debate,
Caught between social studies and the cretic,
Inquires as whether to elucidate
The age, the art, the artist, or the critic –

"Distinctions of these kind are void" (McNeice) –
"Well, three are gonna get their ass whupped" (Sonnet) –
But we're all critics, ("bravo") ("what a piece
Of – "), putting our foot in the mouth with mustard on it,

Until, grades in, you ditch Foucault *and* foot
And overlook the starlet's gown to ex-
plicate the multivalent witticism
In "HERE LIES," that paradox the slow rains put
"Under erasure" to reveal a puzzling text,
"   ," in one last act
                              of criticism.

Line

Lines seem pretty much a necessity
For things like airports, bathrooms, placing a bet,
Cocaine, banks, sonnets, and the DMV
("A line may take us hours maybe, yet")

As you go (asked by various institutions
To walk it, hold it, toe it, and be fed it)
Screwing around with metrical substitutions
In the slim hope of finding a line of credit,

Until the question whether you're the "place
Or the holder" (Robert Schreur) gets left alone
And laurel-less, caesural, you recline
Under the crowning achievement rains erase,
The monumental work, written in stone
And pretty well summed up
                                    in the last line.

Circle

A closed plane curve consisting of the set
Of all – what're you, *Euclid*? spill it – phase,
Used in the manufacture of roulette,
Crop circles, holes, and (aw nuts) this year's raise,

And you've been running in them, chasing your tail; you're
Chief Round Peg, Captain Holding Pattern, Hero
Of Cubicle O, which is the shape of failure,
The life-size manifestation of a zero,

Until, reward for all the overtime,
You finally get that promised office and
A whole new outlook ("hold my calls, Doll, work'll
Wait"), watching buzzards on the thermals climb,
Sipping old fashioneds in vacationland,
That silly old cycle of life having come
                                        full circle.

Square

Back in the 60s, Age of Aquarius,
Peace, flower children, love, and murderous cults,
You had these "Squares," shorn, anti-microbus
Sellouts you might define now as "adults,"

But you were a visionary, stoned, hirsute,
Taking the acid test with Dr. Leary,
Slowly becoming (what a drag) a suit-
And-salary man, rich, Rolexed, and world-weary,

Until ("we're talking 'bout a revolution")
You load up for that last big road trip, see
The South, Deadhead ("there'll be a love-in there"),
Resting in peace and quiet, restitution
For the deal of a lifetime, which turned out to be,
Like your accommodations,
                              fair and square.

Smell

Dogs smell very well, they sniff things out
With *glee* – dead birds, butts, bugs, the garbage can –
But we gross out, won't even talk about
BO, bad breath, feet (*his* feet), farts ("young man!") –

It's *true*! and makes you wonder if your nose
Is in the air because, well, in a word,
Because it *don't* know, as a dog's nose knows,
The underlying *structure* of the turd,

Until your last breath brings back, in a wave,
Those formative first smells – cut grass, the sea,
Sawdust and rain, paint, tar, and coralbell,
The gym on game day, grandpa's aftershave –
Just nosing around, ar*oma therapy*!,
With all the funky junk down here
                                    to smell.

Taco

In poems, the line of *demarcatión*
That separates refined aesthete from cretin
Is that above which there can be no tacos, one
Does not eat tacos, tacos will not be eaten,

But, fastened to a dying animal,
You're made of taco, fear you *are* it, a metrist
Whose range transcends not taco, a shell
Of a man, a maize, a latterday taco belle lettrist,

Until you cant the old sombrero for
A well-deserved siesta, the dingaling
Now lionized, the ragamuffin, cock o'
The walk, with your proleptic metaphor:
A taco of gold and gold enameling,
A fulgent, gong-tormented, gilt
                    Ur-taco.

Beer

A mildly alcoholic beverage
Made from a malted, farinaceous grain
Combined with choice hops and allowed to age,
Beer's "proof God loves us" (Franklin), and we'd fain

Have beer, beer's having given us so much,
Beer bong, beer gut and goggles, beer-induced
Liaisons, bless its beery heart – a crutch?
No way, man, (beer me) you are getting *juiced* –

Until you split to meet the great Beer Man,
Himself, it's Party Time (they serve
An ice cold draft) and you're a legend here,
Immortalized in stone, an artisan,
Artiste – the grit, the showmanship, the verve,
And your last words, "Watch this, man.
                                    Hold my beer."

Marijuana

Cannabis sativa, known on the street
As "doobie," "joint," "pot," "ganja," "Mary Jane,"
"Sao Paulo North Slope Trip Weed," affects the seat
Of squaredom and uptightness in the brain,

Dude (dude, don't do it, dude), outrigging the pots
Head pot – the *pothead's head* – with glimmerings
Of X-ray vision that, as Wordsworth puts
It, lets you "see into the life of things,"

Until you take your last hit and exhale
With a spectacular case of the munchies, cotton
Mouth, but riveted, digging the fauna
Down here – Wormdude and Peter Cottontail –
Lost in the J-hole, grinning your ass off, watching
It all ride by, man, high
                  on marijuana.

Spirits

Illegal spirits – moonshine, hillbilly hearse,
Catdaddy, mule back, stump, skullcracker – came
From old Scots-Irish know-how and payment-averse
Tax strategy, and there's a little game

You used to play with it – some friends and you
'd pass around Arlo's Coon Creek Noggin Fuzz,
Then one'd get up and leave and the other two
Would try to figure out which one it was –

Until, dead drunk, you go on down the road
And set in with your Tennessee flat-top box
And Sunday-go-to-meeting clothes ("I hear it's
A jamboree, boys!"), picking a jet-fueled ode
To woe and heartache, rotgut on the rocks,
Flatpicking, festive, and in right
                                    high spirits.

Soul

"Your business (being) to paint the soul," you made
A list, from Robert Browning's monk's astute
"It's vapors done up like a new-born babe"
And Aristotle's notion "it's a flute"

To Nietzsche ("Christian moral quackery"),
Boethius ("dark ruins ruled by chance"),
And Shakespeare ("the soul of man is his clothes"), q.v.
Robert Montgomery ("the soul aspiring pants")

Until, in what is known as metempsychosis,
Your paint-stained, stone-washed soul's slid off and sold
With your estate, thus transmigrating Skoal
Ring and frayed cuff alike by meddlesome hocus
Pocus, as toiling church bell bottoms tolled
Not just for thee,
                    but every living soul.

Body

"Looked at too long, words fail," observed the late
James Merrill in his poem, "b o d y,"
So why, you wonder, "strictly meditate
The thirsty Muse" (John Milton), eh?, why try

Your hand at this, "now warm and cuppable,"
(John Keats) in light of last night's fortune cookie,
"Your lute, what point?" (Apollo) – unclubbable,
Nonlaid – and not just try to get some nookie,

Until "in pastures new" you tote the leader
Board behind the game's great pros, who wow
The cheering gallery, like your new buddy,
Walt, with whom you'd like to say, "Hi, Reader,
Be not too certain I'm not with you now,"
Except for the delicate matter of having
                                        no body.

Hands

A person affected with the syndrome known
As Alien Hand feels "disassociated
From the hand," which has its *own* will, own
Agenda, for which I endure unmitigated

Indignities – the *bathing*, the *shaving*, all manner
Of cheerless fraternizing with that dim,
Sinister "twin" I punish with a hammer –
And try – *Sweet Jesus!* – not to strangle him

Until one last "thumbs up," one final "ciao,"
And free, uncuffed, sprung, manumitted ("G'day"),
I legerdemain it back to fairyland's
Discarnate airs, sneaking a peek at how
Well *he* writes, Bardboy, down in his atelier,
With that big chunk of time
                             he'll have on his hands.

Feet

Before the Ape Canyon Siege of '24,
The Bluff Creek footage, or that mess near Reelfoot,
The Huppa knew *all* about him, *knew the lore*,
pediculum vasticus, the Common Bigfoot,

And you, the sleuth, the *bloodhound*, with your slung pack
Of Sterno cans and doggedness, have combed
The web page, tracked down tips from cul-de-sac
To the Okefenokee, where the Skunk Ape roamed,

Until (all's being revealed that hath been yadda
Yadda hid) you get an *apeçu*
Of vindication, the countryside's *replete*
With Bigfoots, *silly* with em – Alma, Yeti,
Oh-mah-ha, Sasquatch, Seahtick – and you
Got close as, what would you say it was,

six feet?

Hat

Snood, Shako, Tam-o-shanter, Shriner fez
(It's – ssh! – it's *Turkish*), coonskin cap, toupee,
The Pope's ear trumpet (God's lips straight to his),
Spiked pickelhaube, French art fop beret –

And you've worn plenty, haven't you, old drone? –
The Worker Hat, The Daddy Hat, the Loyal-
Knights-of-the-Kings-of-the-Merovingian-Throne
Hat, made of duct tape and aluminum foil –

Until your haberdasher blocks your last
(Stone) hat, and under the cover of "masonry,"
You join the – ssh! – that centuries-old frat,
Keeping the lore, the Templars' secret past,
The undreamt *scale* of the conspiracy –
Mary, the Pope, Grail (*Jesus!*) –

                                under your hat.

Church

First, there's your local church, that's got the steeple,
Three bean salad (for the Trinity),
And most importantly, of course, the leader
Who does talks at the holy end for *thee*,

And then there's *The* Church, nunned-up, on the take,
Who wrote themselves a bible they could sell,
Held papal synods, burned girls at the stake,
And generally made life a living hell,

Until, "madeth to lie in a new pasture,"
You hit the churchyard in your worship clothes –
Witnessing, brother!, conducting your own search
Into the gnostic past, watching the pastor
Lay hands on – mute, inglorious, and close
As it appears you're going to get
                                    to church.

State

First, there's the state, that group of gerrymandered
Districts devoted to the same state seal,
State bird, dog, football team, and happily pandered
To and robbed blind by the crookmobile,

And then there's *the* State, constituted by
Tax hounds, seized property, the Office of Any
Boondoggle'll Do, and the *lax populi*,
E pluribus unum, of which you were one of many,

Until you take that final exit poll,
And in your crucial demographic you
Start making a difference, you *participate*,
Turning up on the state election roll,
Voting like crazy, taking the civic view,
And pulling, like any American would,

for State.

Home

Of course, by "home" we generally mean "asylum,"
The "*loony*bin," "*le shock d'electric hotiél*,"
But it can also mean (and you've passed by um)
"That locus in which one's domestic affections indwell,"

But it's a quota past the company goal,
And you've missed Christmas, on the road, downstate,
Alone, lost, Loman on the totem pole
In the five o'clock shadow of the Motel Eight,

Until – one last hard knock, last foot in the door –
You get decked out for one last swank convention,
See some friends – *aloha, boys! shalom!* –
Relaxed, clean-shaven, eligible for
The gold watch and that long-awaited pension,
And feeling, for the first time,
                                        right at home.

Internet

Invented by Al Gore, the Internet
Is chiefly used to view pornography,
Meet homicidal strangers, day trade, bet
On offshore football, view pornography,

Peruse bar graphs of pop sensation Britney
Spear's permutable décolleté,
And (oh, just pass the crack pipe, okay, Whitney?)
Chat about the life you e-ed away,

Until you download your last stolen file
And Exit Now, Log Off, to retrogress
In the Actual World's Wide Web of spinneret-
Borne spiders, *earth*worms, *bugs*, and stay awhile
In your last known and permanent address,
Your home away from HOME
                              on the Internet.

Road

From ancient Roman times to the Great Frontier,
Roads have provided governments a place
To put their surplus potholes, cull the deer,
And stage the California High Speed Chase,

And you've knocked deer off miles of them, have clattered
Over so many high spots lane changes you made are
Taught in traffic school and troopers are flattered
In using *you* to calibrate their radar

Until a life on the road and the long haul
Come to an end, *ten-four*, and you let go
The blear commute, the loneliness, the load,
And chill out as your convoy's running all
The red lights to a charming bungalow
Down to the left
                  on Cemetery Road.

Trains

From Stephenson's "LOCOMOTIVE," as he'd call
His "Iron Horse," to *The Best Friend of Charleston*,
Orange Blossom Special, *Wabash Cannonball*,
You loved them, *Zephyr*, *Flyer*, *Burlington*,

The Chief, *The Twentieth Century Limited*,
And the thrilling notion of "a roundhouse right"
When as a boy you lay awake in bed
And listened to them thunder into night,

Until you climb aboard that train that Warren
Zevon calls *When All Is Said And Done* –
The grainy final scene, the lost campaigns –
And find your private sleeping car (where's Lauren
Bacall when you need her?), making your last run,
The Real McCoy from the bygone age
                                        of trains.

Jets

From the Bell X-1 (just after World War II)
To Mach-11 Scramjet prototypes,
Designers dream of slicing up the blue
Empyrean in turd-like tapered pipes,

And there you are, at cruising altitude,
Between a mauve, upchucky Scream Appliance,
A logorheic Aunt Bea in a snood,
And your long, weekly hadj of grim compliance

Until you pull the curtain and ("Holy Cow,
Dude, look at all the legroom") upgrade to
A brand new social caste, with festive fetes
Of rare wild mushrooms, pheasant, curaçao,
Up at the spit-shined pointy end where you
Recline, stretch out, nod off,
                              and cool your jets.

The Blues

"I woke up da da dum this morning da da dum" and...*finis*,
And that's the heart of The Blues, this waking up,
This shaving the face and finding where the gin is,
And the long staring in the coffee cup

In whose black mouth you see the daily grind,
The bitter stirrings of another week,
The ark go down which is itself the mind,
A minnow flipping in the world's hard beak,

Until (Goodnight, Irene) it finds you well
In Avalon in paley pall, the cough
And heartache melting in flat thirds and dews
With Muddy Waters, Hurt, and Blind McTell
In the backwoods speakeasy where you shrugged off
This mortal coil and lifelong case
                              of The Blues.

Music

"From Bix to Buxtehude to Boulez,"
From Dickie Betts to ... *boy bands*? music is
(Ok, we're in a slump, whatever pays)
The bread of life, shoes, soft drinks, and Show Biz,

But far from promises of endless love,
Chrome wheel rims, and eternal youth, the dues
Get paid, dreams die, and there's the music of
Your real life, the walking twelve-bar blues,

Until that golden oldie, *Taps*, is played,
And in a small club in the Underground
You find a new groove, a funky soul-rock fusion –
The daring rests, the breathless solo laid
On lowdown rhythms – it's a timeless sound –
And you kick back, and grin,
                                      and face the music.

Rock

When Seger's unironical ads remind
Us Chevy trucks are "starting from the gate,
Like a rock," buyers better bear in mind
That rocks don't, for the most part, ambulate,

Don't move at, for the most part, all, although
They can be dropped, rolled, added to soup, and thrown
In the glass house you live in, Smartass, Know-
It-All, snide, mendicant *Wisecrackophone*,

Until you're rocked, one final time, to sleep,
Becoming an expert on the sediments –
Slate, sandstone, mudstone – chip off the old block,
Doing the scratch test under (and pretty deep),
"Not marble nor the gilded monuments,"
But just your plain old, personalized
                                        pet rock.

Paper

Deriving from *papyrus*, paper's used
For wrapping gifts, fish, flowers ("azaleas and so on")
And writing odeies, generally excused
As "paper training," merely something to go on,

And you've been on a lifelong paper chase,
Old Rhymeraner, filling out the forms
(Da dum ...) on the thick stack and in the wrong place
"In a lifetime of standing out in thunderstorms,"

Until, old fashioned, out of step, passé,
You get your walking papers and set out
For LANGUAGE school and the slick sign's latest caper,
A clubbable dead white male from the hey-
day, having (halving?) second thoughts about
That little thing you wrote one time
                                    on paper.

Scissors

No *philosophe*, wrestling with the Fates,
Whose old crone Spinster Atropos extends
"The glittering Forfex," underestimates
"The little Engine on [her] Fingers' Ends,"

But Life's got you in (one out of, well, *one* falls)
Locked in the scissors hold, blue in the face,
The paisley hero Tony Earley calls
Lord Poetry, "since mourning doth thee grace,"

Until (oh no) she gets you in the sleeper
Hold and you go down for the (long) count,
Hit with a folding chair by those Three Sisters,
As you and your arch-foes – Stone Cold, The Reaper,
Widow Maker – chummily recount
The brash days when you ran around
                                    with scissors.

Dreams

In bed with Mom, check, Dad's a lizard – why
Ya ask, doc? From Solomon to Shirley MacClaine –
The deep, subconscious structure of the "I,"
Random synaptic spark, or just your plain

Old basic psychic phenomenon – dreams are big
Business, big! – the pharaoh, *Finnegan's Wake*,
Queen Mab, that little matter of the fig
Leaf (kinda makes you want to stay awake) –

Until (night night) you slip into a world
Of dreams, "the children of an idle brain" –
The neighbor girl in skin-tight jeans, the streams
Of visitating angels ("tea?"), those pearled
Front gates – your own Lost Island of Cockaigne,
A well-dressed man of leisure
                              in your dreams.

Salt

A dissociative, ionic substance, salt
Is used to bring back zombies from the dead,
Corn beef, do navel shots, so from the Baltic
Sea to Avery Island, salt's the bread

Of life, old salt, old *soldier*, as you brake
Down 95, the old *Salaria Way*,
To punch the salt mine's clock by nine to make
The salary you can't quite salt away,

Until, a seasoned vet, your salad days
Long gone, you sign up at the old folks' home,
Taking a measure of the new Gestalt,
Practicing Zen, enjoying the holidays
And the cold wind's transcendental "Om,"
And just about precisely
                                        worth your salt.

Pepper

Essential in making jalapeno poppers,
Bloody Marys, and Go-To-The-Mountain-To-Meet-
The-Blue-Coyote salsa, chili peppers
Are ranked in Scoville units as to heat,

Bells being zero, habaneros, +
300,000, as you calculate
The spice in *your* life, Scotch Bonnet, boarding the bus,
Filing, dreaming, dieting, staying late,

Until, deep in the hole, in the field of green,
You watch the boys of summer get their looks –
Satchmo, The Say Hey Kid, The Yankee Clipper,
And Pete Rose ("I'd walk through hell in a gasoline
Suit to keep playing baseball"), eyeing the lanky rook's
Slick glove-work in a hot little game
                                        of pepper.

Gold

Doge, Coronado, and the Klondike Kats,
From Blackbeard, Sutter, and Mel Fisher's missions
To dive Atocha (and duck the bureaucrats)
To that touched Dutchman in the Superstitions

We've got it – gilt-, pelf-, ducat-, blingblingitis –
The gold bug, even after all those years
Of finding you're a sort of anti-Midas,
The golden fleeced, the last of the pyriteers,

Until, gold dust to dust, a flash in the pan,
With mineral rights you stake a small, new claim
And strike it rich in the rich loam, the cold
Coin of the realm, paydirt, a self-made man
Under the secret stone that bears your name,
Buried, inert, refined,
                 and good as gold.

Big Oil

Until we get our telekinetic, solar-
Powered jet packs in a couple years,
We've got the two-ton, fuel-injected stroller
Because when you're rickshawing Suze from Sears

To Soccer on your lunch break you can't use
Your cell phone ("stop that back there!"), so we're stuck
With Oil, *Big* Oil, and everyone has views
On that, but till we get the jet packs, truck,

Until you pack it in for one last car
Ride to the country ("oh, would you look at the flowers")
And, as the continents collide, recoil,
Inch back to sea, you are the avatar
Of Patience and, through ice age and spring showers,
Do your small, selfless part to *be*
                              Big Oil.

Dinosaurs

At the K-T boundary, dinosaurs, whose name,
"Fierce lizards," comes from (*someategrass*), well, yes,
But (*sizeofbunnies*), true, but all the same,
They all became extinct, and our best guess

Is that some cataclysmic meteor
Or geo-(*whatabougators*?) – no, and as
We saw last week – (*bigcrocs*?) – evolved *before*
The – (*Grendel*?) What?! (*My Lit I TA says* –)

Until you don the robes for the faculty roast,
The grand old (*whataboubirds*?) the old alum,
Having gone the way of disco, Dinah Shore's
Last film, and all (*likebobwhitebirds*?), like most
(*likecassowaries*?), fine, goddammit!, some,
Having gone the way of *some*
                                    of the dinosaurs.

Easter Island

The statues, we now know, were carved in place, then
Transconveyed across (some thirteen tons)
The lonely, trade-wind-whipped terrain by spacemen
Using laser beams (see Williamson's

The Secret Places of the Lion), but
That's science, and you contemplate, out there
In mid-Pacific, the obsessive glut
Of clenched jaws and the thousand-mile stare

Until, your excavations at an end,
You see, with peerless eyes, the oblong sun
Go down, and see in your own rocky highland,
Its leaning headstones and the endless wind,
Resigned, enisled, cut off from everyone,
Your kinship with the tribe
                              of Easter Island.

Pyramid

The pyramids, like the lines at Nazca, Peru,
Were built, as Mali's Dogon tribe knows, in
"The lost time by the amphibious Nomo," who
Arrived from Sirius B, "Dog Star's dark twin,"

And, while that's well known now, through years of Rand
McNally maps and ridicule, you knew,
You *knew* the pod bay door would open and
A Spacefishman get out to *talk* to *you*

Until the rains roll in and you collapse
The battered tripod, throw the coffee out,
To watch the splendid Nomo reappear amid
Cold starlight as millenia elapse
Beneath – you old enthusiast, ya *scout* –
Your roughhewn, exclusive, (rectangular),

very own pyramid.

Mountains

Up lateral moraine, arête, cirque, crest –
From Ovid onward mountains have been touted
As symbolizing the poetic quest
("And there's a story in a book about it"),

But looks like you, who made of, in the long run,
Mountains molehills and of molehills mountains
"Of huge despair," (aw nuts) climbed up the wrong one,
No muse here, no Pegasus, no fountains,

Until, "deceived into thinking that you have progressed,"
You send the Sherpa packing and in lieu
Of laurels, in the shadow of the mountains,
Find a plain, pine sounding board to rest
On, listening, with a sense of privilege, to
The "old and solemn harmony"
                                        of mountains.

Mega Tsunami

When Cumbre Vieja hits the ocean floor,
It will create a wave, models have found,
Wider, taller than, and heading for
Manhattan at – oh, ballpark? – speed of sound,

Spreading disease, plague, trench foot, famine, strife,
And "no land" clear to the Blue Ridge Parkway, and you,
Why you're, in the sausagefest you call a life,
Ragdolled and munched, you sabagedbakook, by *dew*

Until – gray suits, Church of the Open Sky –
You take your last sandfacial, caddy a board,
And lay back – though it'll take a helluva swami
To see ya – manning a slab in the boneyard, to ri –
To *rip* that redonculous, that *crazy* good
One thousand-foot-high face
                         of the mega tsunami.

The Ten Spacetime Dimensional Universe

Whether beyond the customary four
Dimensions we live in are six or (get
This!) *seven* more the cosmos has in store
For us, the calibrations aren't in yet

To add to our own inwrought secret spaces,
Reimannian hearts, warped dreams, the dark, abiding
Energy that's bathing our blank faces,
Bathing the whole big brane shebang we's riding

Until, remaindered, factored out, you leave
The numbers game and all you have to show em,
The enlaced rhyme's lamentable, loony verse,
To sail the trillion years it takes to achieve
Absolute Zero in (for the sake of the poem)

The *ten* spacetime dimensional universe.

The Hubble Constant

Where $Ho=v/d$,
The future readership (hi Mark) will no
Doubt know (and smile at our disproficiency)
The value to a parsec of Ho,

But till then you can't date the universe,
Though estimates are ranging from (don't scoff)
Six thousand years to twenty billion, diverse
Conclusions probably from rounding off,

Until the old observatory dome
Door closes and you catch on as a guest
In the sinuous rills of the long, untroubled Khan's stint
In fertile Xanadu – "that sunny dome!
Those caves of ice!" – as fixed, as laid to rest,
As buried as, perhaps,
                        the Hubble Constant.

Light

Like light can be stretched by space, like there's no aether –
The particle-wave duality, the "sum-
Over-paths" delusions Feynman yoked together –
It's one big dodge, man, I mean just how dumb –

But you, the dupe, the *stooge*, are in the dark,
Blind to the Franklins in the paper sack,
The graft, the corporate fronts (a self-made mark),
The water cooler talk behind your back,

Until your eyes are opened and you see
The *solace* of the dark, its ebon air,
The katydids' and bullfrogs' recondite
Aesopics, and your suave obscurity –
Hermetic, undercover, out of the glare
And glad, *brightened*, having seen, that is,
                                        the light.

Black

Blacked-out reports of "a crashed disc," the Feds'
Filmed autopsies, eyewitness stories spun
As hoaxes, all those craft the figureheads
In State dismiss as "swamp gas," "plovers," "the sun – "

And you, the nut, the *dreamer*, with your black eye
Have scoured the cover-up (see Project Blue
Book, MJ-12) and that vast, bustling sky,
Thermos on STUN, to glimpse the rendezvous

Until, just outside town, in a remote field,
You are abducted from your car ("just froze,
I guess") to be observed ("no, *on* my back")
By a crack team and the High Priest, revealed
As having chosen *you* to join all those
Elusive, "odd-complexioned" men
                                        in black.

White

"Only when we kick the habit of mind
Which sees in pictures little corners of nature,
Madonnas, shameless Venuses shall we find
A work of living art," saith the lecture,

And you, the hack, the *scribbler*, with your dumb grin
Of sentiment, sign, self, the vulgar heart
Of content, tint, *text*, were complicit in
The well-patinaed, off-white lies of art

Until, in your clean (last) white shirt so chic
Down here, through reams of winters, you pursue
Your final undertaking, to ghostwrite,
In air, a palimpsest of pure technique,
Stripped of allusion, mediation, you:
Moonlight on Snow with Wind in White
                                    on White.

Index of Titles and First Lines

A Note About the Author

Greg Williamson grew up in Nashville, Tennessee. His first book, *The Silent Partner*, was published by Storyline Press and won the Nicholas Roerich Prize in 1995. His second book, *Errors in the Script*, was published by Overlook Press in 2001 and was runner-up for the NYC Poets' Prize. He has received a Whiting Award, an NEA grant, and an Academy Award in Literature from the American Academy of Arts and Letters, among other honors. He teaches in The Writing Seminars at Johns Hopkins University.

Other books from Waywiser